Friction Fuel

The Secret to Listening Strategically
and Leveraging Complaints to Keep
Your Business Running on Premium

Other Books by Chad Jenkins

Just Add a Zero: Remove the Film, Outperform your Competition, and Grow Exponentially through Collaboration

Friction Fuel

The Secret to Listening Strategically
and Leveraging Complaints to Keep
Your Business Running on Premium

Chad T. Jenkins

SEEDSPARK
COLLECTIVE

Published by Igniting Souls
PO Box 43, Powell, OH 43065
IgnitingSouls.com

LCCN: 2024918995
Paperback ISBN: 978-1-63680-383-8
Hardcover ISBN: 978-1-63680-384-5
e-book ISBN: 978-1-63680-385-2

Available in paperback, hardcover, e-book, and audiobook.

Any Internet addresses (websites, blogs, etc.) and telephone numbers printed in this book are offered as a resource. They are not intended in any way to be or imply an endorsement by Igniting Souls, nor does Igniting Souls vouch for the content of these sites and numbers for the life of this book.

Some names and identifying details may have been changed to protect the privacy of individuals.

The superscript symbol IP listed throughout this book is known as the unique certification mark created and owned by Instant IP™. Its use signifies that the corresponding expression (words, phrases, chart, graph, etc.) has been protected by Instant IP™ via smart contract. Instant IP™ is designed with the patented smart contract solution (US Patent: 11,928,748), which creates an immutable time-stamped first layer and fast layer identifying the moment in time an idea is filed on the blockchain. This solution can be used in defending intellectual property protection. Infringing upon the respective intellectual property, i.e., IP, is subject to and punishable in a court of law.

Cover Designed by Prismo Marketing

Contents

An Open Letter to the Readers of *Friction Fuel*

Dear Reader,

When I first introduced the concept of Remove the Film in *Just Add a Zero*, it wasn't just a framework—it became the lens through which I've navigated every opportunity and challenge. Remove the Film taught me that friction is inevitable but also essential. It's the tension that fuels transformation. This principle not only shaped my journey but has empowered countless entrepreneurs to unlock their potential by embracing friction.

With *Friction Fuel*, I want to take this concept even further—because growth is no longer an individual pursuit. It's a collaborative effort.

This book is about more than just identifying and resolving friction; it's about leveraging the collective power of collaboration to fuel exponential growth. The Friction Operating System (FOS) I've developed is designed not only to address friction within your own organization but to invite collaboration from a global community of entrepreneurs. It's a system that turns challenges into opportunities, aligning vision, capability, and action across teams and networks.

Through my work with SEEDSPARK Growth Partners, I've witnessed firsthand how powerful collaboration can be when combined with friction. It's also why my team and I created CoLAB—a digital platform where entrepreneurs from around the world can come together, share their friction points, and collectively transform them into innovative solutions. CoLAB isn't just about connecting businesses; it's about building a global collaborative community where visionaries push boundaries, solve problems, and accelerate growth through shared experiences.

Friction doesn't just create opportunities—it builds a culture of continuous innovation. It encourages collaboration at every level, where diverse perspectives fuel new ideas, and collective strengths drive breakthrough solutions. The FOS is your framework for tapping into this power—not just within your organization but by joining a global network of like-minded entrepreneurs ready to turn friction into fuel.

Whether you're just starting out or you're guiding a team of experienced innovators, *Friction Fuel* will empower you to see friction not as a roadblock but as an engine for collaboration, innovation, and lasting success.

Thank you for being part of this journey. Together, we'll harness the power of friction to fuel growth far beyond what any of us could achieve alone.

Warm regards,
Chad Jenkins

Finding the Fountain of Endless Friction Fuel

FROM THE TIME I turned six, regardless of the weather, it was my job to haul buckets of grain to twenty to thirty horses early each morning and again after I got home from school. I didn't mind going to the barn when the temperatures rose above freezing, but from December through March, that one hour every morning felt like three. It took as long to bundle up as it did to feed the animals. And in the winter before school, the sun didn't show up to keep us warm. Did you know it's impossible to break the ice on the top of a watering trough without getting soaking wet—especially when you're only three-and-a-half feet tall? So, after I finished my chores, I had to change into something dry before I walked to the end of the long driveway to stand in the cold and wait on the bus. By the time I got to my first grade desk, I was chilled to the bone.

Now, before you come down too hard on my parents for sending such a little guy out to take care of barn chores, I want to assure you that this is just part of farm life. The folks I know who were raised in that environment appreciate all they learned from the experience—even the ones who don't want to keep on farming. For me, in addition to developing a tremendous work ethic, the trust my family put in me to carry out my responsibilities gave me confidence and increased my self-worth. Plus, every single thing I did on the farm fed my curious nature and set me on the path to discovering the primary lesson I want to share with you—how to turn friction into a powerful and invaluable fuel for value creation.

Friction has been propelling me forward for more than four decades. I started by seeing a way to give sellers at horse auctions an advantage at age eight, and then I cornered the market on bush-hogging empty lots for banks at sixteen. Each of the dozens and dozens of companies I've started was born out of and grew rapidly using Friction Fuel. Over the years, I have discovered the best ways to drill for this free and renewable energy source. And now, I thrive on showing others how to optimize the Friction Operating System[IP] (FOS).

In case you're wondering, I did find a little fuel for my cold weather friction. I prepared the grain the night before so I didn't have to be out so long in the coldest part of the day, and I trained the horses to get into their stalls a bit quicker. Not bad for a six-year-old, right?

Part One: Complaints

Chapter 1

Running on Regular

FARMS, LIKE LIFE, ARE full of obstacles. But as Ryan Holiday pointed out in his best-selling book, *The Obstacle is the Way*, when we learn to see obstacles as opportunities and friction as fuel, we begin to look for things we can learn in the middle of every frustration.

I remember shortly after I turned eleven, we returned home from a horse sale and found the gate open. Knowing I hadn't been the one to forget to hook the latch gave me only a moment of relief because at one in the morning, who didn't close it doesn't matter. Forty horses outside the fencing meant every available hand worked to track down the herd. No one went to bed until we had them all back in the pasture. I went to school pretty tired the next morning. The ordeal prompted me to help other farmers avoid that friction.

One of my first adult ventures was a farm and equine supply store. By offering solutions for equine owners and other farmers, I quickly became the largest paneling gate distributor in the Carolinas. Even in my early twenties, I tried to remember the lessons friction taught me, so obviously, automatic gate enclosures topped my list of things to include in the inventory.

In my first book, *Just Add a Zero*, I revealed the value of FILM[IP] (Friction Identification and Leverage the Market). Removing the FILM has become one of my driving secrets to creating unique value in many different industries—even those in which I had no prior history. Industry evolution is inevitable. And it pays well to be the catalyst of evolution. Plus, it's easier than you might guess.

From as far back as I can remember, I actively looked for ways to alleviate the friction or leverage it to create something better. While everyone else runs away from difficulty, I ask questions until I get to the root of the problem, then find ways to create value from what I learn. I'm not even sure I realized my process was so unique until I saw other entrepreneurs struggle to embrace the negativity.

Walk Into the Wind

An ancient Irish blessing says, "May the wind be always at your back." And while that's a more comfortable way to walk, it's not a productive way to innovate business. If we refuse to walk into the wind and embrace the friction, the problems, like the wind at our back, will push us—and not necessarily in the direction we want to go.

Windmills have provided industrialists with energy for millennia. Persians first realized if you are willing to face the wind head-on, you can harness its power. Grinding grain, creating powders, and pumping water have long been automated because someone understood the importance of walking into the wind.

Complaints and problems are the unlimited wind available in the business world. But let's face it, we don't like to hear complaints. It's much easier to give them a listen, resolve them, and move on. Entrepreneurs often have to handle the friction so quickly that they miss the deeper-rooted issue. Many times, the criticism doesn't even make it to their desk until it's too late, and a few prefer to pass it off and go into the next meeting or a new project. The sound of problems creates tension and anxiety. Some business owners will put off solving them until the dam breaks. They keep pushing through and putting the complaints in their back pocket until three people start knocking at the door, and the inbox fills up. Eventually, the friction causes a festering sore.

Like the wind, this unpleasant but inevitable part of business can be your growth's best friend or your worst enemy. You can harness the friction as a powerful source of energy and innovation, or you can let it push you in unpredictable and destructive directions. Unfortunately, some choose a third option.

Bandages and Fire Extinguishers

Yes, a third alternative exists. It's the one a significant number of business owners choose, but it's not any more sustainable than ignoring the disharmony. Making quick fixes without delving into the true source of the mess is like pulling weeds. If you don't dig up the roots, they'll just come back and create more havoc later.

Too many look at the surface of the situation. They fix the immediate or address the urgent, but just like trying to use a bandage for a broken arm or a fire extinguisher for a major blaze, while this method may appear to alleviate the pain, it simply prolongs it.

Sakichi Toyoda developed a technique I have expanded upon to avoid bandage and fire extinguisher fixes. He recommends taking a deep dive into why the problem surfaced in the first place. Toyoda said, "By repeating why five times, the nature of the problem as well as its solution becomes clear." I take it one step further and also dig deep into the five whos.

This process, I call the 5x5 Method[IP], will help you get to the bottom of the reason something is happening as well as who it will ultimately affect. When I started practicing Toyoda's technique, I often ran into issues when I got to the root because when I began to implement, I realized I had to then consider all the people everything I had learned would affect. This prompted me to add the five whos to my system. Sometimes, I'll only need to dive down three or four levels, but often, when I get to what appears to be the end, I ask one more why and who and discover an answer I'd never imagined.

Because I tend to be relentlessly curious, the process comes naturally to me, but even those who don't have this innate trait can use Toyoda's technique to discover which small underlying modification can tip the scales significantly to yield a much bigger outcome. Without asking why, entrepreneurs—men and women who typically have grandiose and marvelous ideas—will make big changes that create tsunami-style waves throughout the company.

It's like the woman who always cut the roast in half to cook it. When her husband asked why, she said, "Because my mother always did it that way." Her husband didn't think that was an extremely valid answer. So, the young bride asked her mother why. Her mother replied, "Because my mother always did it that way." Still not satisfied, the woman asked her grandmother. Grandmother replied, "Because I never had a pot big enough to cook a whole roast." One or two whys did not sufficiently solve the problem. But in this case, it took only three to realize the answer to the friction was a bigger pot for Grandma.

Diving deep into the five whys and whos also keeps me from looking like a buffoon. Before I forge ahead with a huge fix, I vet them in my head or with a select audience until I reach the ocean floor. Occasionally, when you search beneath the top layer, you discover the reason for the process is because it's the best way for it to be in existence, and a change will negatively impact too many whos. In that case, though the surface tension makes a few folks uncomfortable, modifications will disrupt the entire Eco structure. Change for the sake of change is as debilitating as a cast on an arm that simply needs a bandage.

What Kind of Fuel Are You Running On?

The way you view complaints and problems determines the kind of fuel your business runs on. Those who rely on bandages and fire extinguishers see every criticism and challenge as something to avoid or run from. Void of the Five Whys and Whos and a strategic way to embrace those criticisms and challenges, they find themselves running on Regular Friction Fuel[IP]. Their extinguishers work overtime because even their hair is on fire. I hear a number of examples from companies running on Regular.

- Our pipelines are drying up.
- We see less and less revenue.
- Renewals are down.
- Attrition is through the roof.
- Our best talent keeps walking out the door.

Regular grade friction is clearly the kind you and your team feel. It forces you to react. Even if you're trying your best to be a little proactive, you end up reacting proactively to the consistency of complaints. And avoidance or applying bandages just makes them multiply more quickly. They come in at a department level, supplier level, product level, and systems level. These companies meet few Milestones per Growth Cycle[IP] (MPG).

I find it interesting that most companies and cultures around the world count each ninety-day period as a growth cycle. A quarter without upward movement can be deadly to a business. To that end, I set five milestones for each three-month period—three impactful and large goals that are practically non-negotiable to meet and two bonus milestones so I'm prepared for those quarters when things move quickly and allow me to celebrate along the way. Those who neglect setting MPGs watch their team leave exhausted at the end of the day, and they end up dealing with extreme employee turnover.

These low MPG business owners know they can't win the race because they simply don't have enough fuel to finish, and their profit and loss reports show it. Their activity level looks good, but they don't have the numbers to show for it. If you feel as though you spend most of your time and energy playing catch up, you're running on Regular, and your supply is probably running low.

Companies that run on Plus Friction Fuel[IP] have begun to see those complaints as opportunities and tools. These businesses understand the value of the obstacles, but they haven't figured out how to harness them yet. They are done with the bandages and fire extinguishers—at least most of the time; however, they know their MPG could be better. Often, the businesses I see running on Regular Friction Fuel started out with mid-grade energy; however, when complaints seemed minor, they brushed them off. They haven't implemented any means to capture the friction or strategically quantify it to make the most direct impact on their innovations. I have observed that it only takes about three months of ignoring friction to lose ground and move back to Regular Friction Fuel.

Many entrepreneurs I consult with around the world run on Plus. They collaborate with me because they want to optimize their ability to create value and embrace competitive advantages, resulting in exponential growth. Looking for better retention rates for their team as well as their clients, these companies have a vision; they just need to learn how to Remove the FILM[IP] to really begin to leverage their capability to create an industry of one.

I have a passion to help entrepreneurs create businesses that run on Premium Friction Fuel[IP]. Let's face it: with so many humans involved, there will always be complaints, criticisms, obstacles, and complications. We can't stop them, but we can harvest and manufacture them into something bigger and better—something that propels our companies forward and provides a catalyst for unlimited growth. And if we don't learn how to capitalize on the friction, even companies who run on Premium will lose the opportunity to reach their full potential. Some will even lose momentum and end up running on Regular Friction Fuel within a year. Embracing mindsets and methods to run on Premium Friction Fuel is a game changer.

Every company I've created and each innovation I've developed for others has originated in friction. I identify the Friction and Leverage it to bring something new to life. And one of my rules is the new creation can't simply benefit me; it has to benefit and bring value to others. This is the real secret of Premium Friction Fuel. Doing my best to make other businesses' and individuals' lives better will give me the most MPG from my time and energy. This philosophy is the reason I absolutely love getting up and going to work every morning. Premium Friction Fuel does more than just improve your business and increase your productivity; it has the power to add joy to your life. You began to see the world of business as a playground of four-dimensional chess.

Every entrepreneur needs and has the ability to optimize the FOS and run their business on Premium Friction Fuel. It will take a bit of work to mine it, but once you hit the reservoir, if you keep following the process, you'll have a never-ending supply of ways to create unique and competitive advantages in your industry. It's time to give up the bandages and fire extinguishers of Regular Friction Fuel and find the energy that will take you to the next level. Let me introduce you to the complete Friction Operating System.

Part Two: Capability

Chapter 2

Learning to Listen Strategically

THE NUMBER ONE INGREDIENT of Premium Friction Fuel is the ability to listen and develop an awareness of the slightest deviation from optimal performance. After working with entrepreneurs from around the world, I've recognized that regardless of culture, these men and women are primarily the first to recognize a friction in their company and their industry. I've furthermore noticed that smaller organizations making changes in an attempt to scale often hold on to what exists, not because they enjoy doing the work, although some do, but because they fear losing access to the voice of the people they want to be a hero to. What if they grow to the point they can't use their spidey sense to recognize those Premium and Plus frictions?

Alleviating that fear is why I built the Friction Operating System[IP]—a process any organization can implement. I set out to create a method that would free up entrepreneurs by providing a way to empower their organization's hero targets to participate in value creation and innovation. FOS takes immense responsibility off the entrepreneur and gives them the capacity to deliver their unique value contribution rather than spend their valuable time trying to spot trends. You see, when we begin to embrace complaints as a leveraging advantage and listen to those who are engaged in our business, we will see an upgrade in the fuel our businesses run on. And the best part is it requires no more work. In fact, it actually lightens your load. FOS easily captures friction and leverages AI to identify what your leadership should focus on to create the greatest value for the people who matter most. FOS allows your organization to start looking at those criticisms as pieces of gold. Your entire team begins to create a competitive advantage by simply listening to those you serve.

Reform Your Inbox

The first step in running on FOS is to reform your listening strategy by creating a new shared email inbox. Allow Friction@YourCompanyWebsite.com (where YourCompanyWebsite points to your domain) to collect complaints and problems. Give the address to every client, vendor, and team member and encourage them to send an email every time they run across some friction. Don't forget to set up an auto-reply so the sender knows their message has been received. This automation also provides an awesome way to set expectations of what comes next.

Not only do you give your most important people a voice, but you now have a dumping ground for friction, and it costs you nothing. This means every problem gets logged. When the receptionist hears a criticism, she simply sends a message to your Friction inbox. If your service technician runs into a problem in the field or has a comment from a dissatisfied customer, he doesn't have to remember to tell someone, who then has to pass the friction up the chain. Instead, he quickly sends a message, perhaps as a text, and the issue will be automatically added to the list.

Now, in order to turn this into a listening tool, once a week, we transfer all those email messages into a spreadsheet and then feed them into an AI review. Rather than trying to keep track of trends as the complaints come in, you can look at the big picture. As you add to your list, you can see which problems keep emerging.

I've created some prompts I use in ChatGPT to quickly spot trends in your friction. For instance, "The following upload contains recent frictions identified by my team at <yourcompanyname>. Our website is <yourcompanyname. com>. Please identify the top ten trends found in this group of frictions. We intend to use these to listen to the voice of our clients (or team or supply partners) to process them with our leadership at our next meeting. Please consider our mission, core values, and position in the marketplace. Also, please rank them in order of impact based on value created for our respective Hero Targets." If you'd like a full list of the prompts I use, visit SeedSpark.com/AI-Prompts.

After I get results for one week, I expand my uploaded list to include two weeks, four weeks, a quarter, six months, and a year. This is the beauty of AI. We humans have a hard time quickly digesting data, but computers, specifically AI, are made to do that instantly and much more effectively. We're good at taking the data outcome and becoming creative with it; that's why AI won't replace us. However, using it as a tool can help us easily see which problems keep appearing and allow us to make informed strategic decisions. Then, by applying the Five Whys to get to the root of the issue and using the Five Whos to identify the number of parties impacted, this AI-generated list can become useful in your next leadership meeting. You can better understand who you need to communicate with and how you'll share information. Often, we find the answer to our friction from the input of our Whos. Then we'll know what needs to be included in the solution to most quickly implement the new FOS creation. The outcome of this strategy results in the most impactful and fastest implementation of solutions to fuel our businesses.

Premium Friction Fuel means we're more efficient while providing even greater value, moving us way ahead of our competition with ease. This one step gives us access to unlimited innovation, and our method of solution vetting ensures rapid adoption by everyone affected.

Listen to Your Hero Target

It's easy to get so involved with the running of our businesses that we become out of tune with our Hero Target. I was originally introduced to this concept by Dan Sullivan. Often, entrepreneurs reference the person they build their businesses around as their "Target Clients." When I heard Dan mention Hero Target, I immediately thought about the many different profiles my businesses Hero Targets have. In an instant, I immediately thought of the obvious: the client. But then the rest became very clear. The list includes the teams in each of my businesses, as well as my suppliers and vendors—from the 401k providers to the people who clean the office. Embracing each of these people individually and sharing with them the way we create and how we remove friction with our businesses has been a complete shift in our existence. Each of our Hero Targets drives our overall success and limits our regular friction. We don't have to change suppliers or find new cleaning crews in the middle of a busy season.

To define all the types of Hero Targets in your business, Dan says to ask yourself one specific question: Who do I want my business to be a hero to? This won't be a huge list, but it will be more than you might expect. Then, we have to understand the needs of each type of person. That's what makes our Friction email inbox so valuable. It allows us to know each of our Hero Targets better and better. SEEDSPARK's client Hero Target is the growth-minded entrepreneur who is ready to divorce conventional growth trajectory methods in his or her industry. So, this is the person we design all our offerings around. This attracts the best and repels the rest.

When you consider your Hero Targets, it's important to resist the thoughts of what you'll get back out of the equation. Yes, it works reciprocally sometimes. Robert Caldini's awesome book *Influence* accurately describes the law of reciprocity. Still, that can't be the motivation. If you're thinking about what you'll get out of it, are you doing it for them, or are you doing it for yourself? Your motives become inauthentic, and other humans will sense it innately. When we lose focus of this goal, we begin bumping up against the outer bands of our existence because we're not following the right path. If we get back to center on that path of what we were created to do and be—namely, create value for one another—we can move about freely and efficiently. True success comes when we do our part to help someone else with no expectations attached.

When creating the ideal atmosphere for your Hero Targets becomes the goal, complaints look more inviting. We begin to become more intentionally present and look for those criticisms because we understand they are the source of Premium Fuel. I have even been told that entrepreneurs who embrace the FOS mindset start to automatically see frictions everywhere.

People often ask, "What's the easiest way to identify a friction?" It's easier than you might think. The next time you get an email and find yourself doing that miniature shrug—you know, that tightening of your shoulders because the email caused some tension, look at it as an opportunity and forward it to the Friction inbox.

Because your team has the power to use the Friction inbox as well, you've freed them from striving to fix things for the client. Now, your team members can tell your Hero Target they've sent their suggestion to the Friction team. Plus, he or she can give them an assurance that every single item gets looked at weekly. This also allows your team member to let it go and focus on what he or she does best, knowing your organization will be using that email to grow your company through consistent intentional focus on creating value. Your team understands their importance in the value creation process and feels sure their contribution won't just slip away unnoticed.

In surveys we've conducted among teams that use FOS, the results overwhelmingly point to Friction Fuel having a positive impact on company culture. This is over and above the rising customer satisfaction level FOS provides. The impact this system provides speaks to its continuous value.

FOS also allows you and your team to focus on your Hero Targets rather than putting out the fires. When we listen to our Hero Targets, we discover they will show us how to create value for them. We never have to chase trends again. If we encourage our entire organization to embrace this, it will free you to use your brain power and experience to forecast the friction that will affect our Hero Targets before the masses begin to feel it in the industry. Someone will eventually come up with the solution to each piece of friction. Why shouldn't you be the innovator?

You can't create and innovate when you're running on Regular Friction Fuel. Convention—Regular Friction Fuel—chases the fires and lets them direct their motion. Innovation—Premium Friction Fuel—controls the flames by focusing on the smallest spark, recognizing the overall impact of that spark if left to grow. Then, innovation harnesses the spark to create a competitive advantage and increase value. By learning to listen strategically, focusing on your Hero Targets, and providing them with a system to quickly bring problems—real or perceived—to your attention, you stay in front of problems and become a category of one.

Overcome Conventional Thinking

Strategic listening means we move past conventional thinking. Often, as companies grow, they become enamored with the name on the door and fall into the trap of "best industry practices." They might hear them at an association event or read them in an article. Unfortunately, this list of business processes and tactics creates a merely average existence. When you adhere to your industry's best practices, you're conforming. This thinking limits your overall potential and, ultimately, your growth.

For example, the best practices of my first supply store would have included adding farm implements and feed. But even back then, without knowing it, I consistently listened to my Hero Targets. By focusing on them with purpose, I noticed my farm supply customers needed trailers to haul things—including their cattle and horses. With this awareness in mind, I added trailers of every type to my inventory. I quickly recognized I could sell more trailers and increase cash flow if I solved my Hero Targets' need for financing.

Then, I noticed many of my farm supply regulars would get value from the latest in mobile phones, and they didn't want to run all over town to get what they needed. So, I threw convention out the window and opened a Nextel® distributorship in the store. I'd been the kid who rode horses all my life. Everyone associated me with farming, rodeos, and horse training. I never wanted to be called "the phone guy."

Conventional thinking would never turn that Nextel counter into a phone delivery system. But that made it easier for my Hero Targets to do business with me rather than the other retail stores around the city. And if I didn't want to be the phone guy, opening the first Blackberry® store in the world didn't make sense. However, when I realized each client had the information they needed to easily transfer to the field and vice versa, that store became the answer to my Hero Targets' friction.

50" TV created the screen for my
giant-sized Blackberry at the grand opening

Even before I opened the phone store, I recognized more friction. While everyone understood how to use a mobile phone—tap, tap, tap, O—tap tap, N—this was the first device to host a calendar, email, and a full keyboard. So, in order to embrace this friction and create a competitive advantage over everyone else in the market—in fact, in the country—I started Blackberry U with my friend Jim Bailey of Red Moon Marketing. Blackberry thought it was so revolutionary that they even funded some of the store's development.

Conventional thinking would never have embraced all this opportunity. It would have missed the exponential growth the friction provided, as well as the lifelong business relationships this business approach created. Many people who bought feed from me in that first business endeavor remain clients of almost all my businesses.

Friction Fuel: The World's Oldest Renewable Energy Resource

The best and worst part of running on Friction Fuel is the fact you'll never run out. Embracing the friction creates growth, and growth causes more friction. Since the beginning of time, humans have produced an endless supply of resistance. We feel the friction when life gets tough or uncomfortable, and we like it when someone makes things easier. From the invention of the wheel, harnessing fire, and fashioning metal into implements and weapons to wireless phones, fast food, and the internet, Friction Fuel has been at work.

We need to use strategic listening to mine friction like a miner uses a pick or a sieve. Those obstacles are as valuable as gold because, within each one, you'll find more energy and greater power to move forward. Each solution feeds the friction stream because the shift will inevitably disrupt some other person or process, which allows you to create even more fuel. As the cycle continues, so will your pool of friction.

Many look at friction with trepidation. They avoid those complaining emails and put off dealing with negativity. However, friction should be embraced. When we see friction as opportunity, it becomes a catalyst for growth. Friction is

Fuel

Resulting

In

Consistent

Transformative

Innovation

Often

Neglected

Friction Fuel is, in essence, value creation. Every time you turn friction into a process, product, or service, you bring value to the world and your Hero Target. Strategic listening is the first step in becoming a category of one.

Chapter 3

Turning Friction into Premium Fuel Takes Practice

FARM KIDS LEARN TO drive before they turn ten. Tractors and their slow nature make a great precursor to the four-wheel drive trucks needed to haul supplies and check fencing. So, while other parents paid for their teens to have driving lessons, I took my horse skills one step further.

If I had been raised on a horse ranch in Texas or Oklahoma, roping would have been part of my life as a young boy. But that's not a skill horse farmers focus on in the Carolinas. So, when I decided I wanted to compete, I had a significant disadvantage over others who rode the rodeo circuit. I had only one choice if I wanted to catch up.

Every evening after school, I sat a dummy in the middle of the barn and practiced roping from every angle. I threw that rope again and again until I hit that dummy one hundred times in a row. If I missed, the count started over. It's this same kind of repetitive action that will transform your

Regular Friction Fuel identification into Premium Friction awareness.

Develop Awareness of Friction Fuel in Your Industry

Every company launched out of an awareness of friction and continues to run on some kind of Friction Fuel. You're either reacting to the friction, seeing and proactively responding to the trends, or forecasting future frictions from heightened focus and awareness and, therefore, running on Premium. Premium Friction Fuel creates new industries and invites evolution to existing ones because it lets you stay out in front of the pack by constantly increasing the value your organization creates. This type of high-level focus, accompanied by a simple yet extraordinarily valuable system, unveils the potential to remove competition and create your own margin. You are no longer beholden to the conventional returns most in your industry strive for. Those running on Premium stay so in tune with their Hero Targets that they innovate solutions to friction before the masses feel it, enabling them to be the only game in town when the friction spreads to other companies in their industry.

Most organizations never consider embracing frictions. Instead, they seem to intensely focus on their internal working, not paying attention to the impact of friction on those they serve. Companies never run out of Plus Friction Fuel because complaints feed it. Those who make this their main source of energy run a little less efficiently. Instead of staying ahead of the complaints, they act on them; however, because they recognize the friction and adjust accordingly, these businesses will still be able to outpace their competitors. With a bit of tweaking and intention, they'll be able to spot the trends and move up to Premium Fuel.

Your level of awareness of all three types of fuel co-existing in your organization will determine your success. But even if you've considered the concept before, implementing FOS will take the same consistent practice I put into learning to rope.

Systematically embracing the reality of the three types of fuel as an entrepreneur allows you to chart the course and make consistent, impactful changes. This means involving your leadership team and training your managers to carry out the Friction Operating System[IP], so you're able to capture even the smallest degree of friction and leverage AI to determine the trends.

As I learned to rope, I envisioned every move a steer might make. As the conditions changed—rain, snow, cold, smoldering—every factor played into the behaviors alongside the individual differences of each steer. I wanted to be able to predict the animal's thoughts and transitions smoothly, and I had to develop a system to communicate to my horse which way we needed to move next. After I polished my technique, I turned my roping into a collaboration. My teammate and I put in countless hours working out the friction, learning to anticipate each other, and practicing to keep one step ahead of the steer. Our efforts took us to the Team National High School Finals for many years as well as the United States Roping Championships when we were just nineteen. But without that concerted effort to create an astute awareness of our surroundings and the friction around us, we would never have left the Carolinas.

It takes that same kind of practice and intentionality to create awareness of your current level of Friction Fuel. If you allow complacency to set in or begin to settle for good enough, even though when you started your company, you were running on Premium, you'll find yourself filling up with Regular and slowly running out of steam.

Premium Friction Fuel for Your Team

The closer you get to running on Premium Friction Fuel, the more you'll want to ensure that it runs throughout your entire organization. The sensation of high-speed efficiency and operating in your Unique Value Contribution[IP] (UVC) becomes addicting.

While we tend to focus on client complaints, companies running on Premium make team friction an equally high priority. Highly productive entrepreneurs will be quick to tell you a happy team yields happy clients. When everyone in your organization feels heard and valued, they push that sentiment forward. Attrition rates decline, and the atmosphere of your organization becomes more pleasant, even magnetizing, for the best talent.

A team running on Premium Friction Fuel gives the entrepreneur extra time to spend with clients as well as the ability to look outside the conventions of the industry. They can more easily predict potential problems and victories that lie on the horizon.

It's impossible to run a company of more than a couple of people without obstacles—even a family-based business. When high-performing individuals work together, they create friction as naturally as the pistons in your engine. And like your car's engine, when you allow unnecessary friction to continue, you put extra strain on your organization and see a loss of mileage.

Unfortunately, entrepreneurs can create unnecessary friction. Expecting everyone in your organization to operate with an entrepreneurial mindset sets the friction in motion. Even your most entrepreneurial-minded employee won't have the same foresight and innovative thinking you do. If they did, they would probably have started their own company. So, by your non-action, you create unnecessary friction.

Entrepreneurs are more naturally programmed to solve problems all day and reflect on them. Their mindset instantly recognizes the fourth time there has been a question about a supplier or an issue with a delivery. However, having a process or system in place that inexpensively captures these issues empowers your entire team to see the friction more clearly and implement a solution. Otherwise, the entrepreneur constantly gets involved in things he absolutely should not be handling. And before you know it, you've settled for Plus Friction Fuel with the potential to run on Regular hot on its heels.

Giving your team permission to complain constructively is the first step. Encourage them to use your Friction inbox to share internal problems they encounter as freely as they report external problems. Then, train someone to run those trends through AI and apply the 5x5 Principle—digging deep into the Five Whys and the Five Whos. You may even create a new process or two that will work for any company and find a whole new revenue stream or even your next new business. I've experienced this a few times, and it has enabled me to birth new entrepreneurs.

Turn Annoyance into Pronoyance[IP]

Jim Rohn said, "You can have more than you've got because you can become more than you are...Unless you change how you are, you will always have what you've got." A huge part of upgrading to Premium Friction Fuel comes from a mindset shift. Problems turn into potential, complaints become constructs, and annoyances begin to be what I like to call pronoyances[IP].

Most recently, my wife and I and our two girls found ourselves homeless for a time. Not for lack of money—that would have been more than an annoyance. The timeframe for the home we planned to move into shifted so drastically that we sold, closed, and needed to vacate the house we owned before our new home could be finished. Instead of simply packing boxes and moving into a new residence, we had to sort through our belongings and decide what we could live without for a month or so. Those items had to go into storage while the things we needed on a daily basis went with us. The entire ordeal just happened to coordinate perfectly with one of the busiest weekends of our summer.

I had an out-of-town meeting as well as a remote meeting the minute my plane touched down. Plus, we had to pick our girls up from camp and then find a place to stay for two days before I flew out again, and the rest of my family went to our vacation home. We had arranged to rent a house as soon as we returned so we could prepare for back-to-school, and eventually found ourselves moving from one Airbnb to another until our new home was ready.

Not one piece of that experience is earth-shattering or life-altering. On the other hand, the inconvenience had the potential to be extremely annoying. My wife and I could have allowed the stress to produce Regular Friction Fuel—bickering, short tempers, and general irritation. And you and I both know our children would have picked up the vibe and created even more misery. Instead, we chose to look at the next few months of disruption as an adventure—a pronoyance.

A pronoyance has the ability to cause irritation and disruption. However, a slight shift in mindset turns it into something better, even pleasant. In our case, it brought a grand adventure. And we all know annoyances come in unlimited supply. There's a never-ending river of complaints, criticisms, and complications. The secret to conquering the friction and turning it into value lies in how we look at them.

For example, even my girls joined me in harnessing the friction of our pronoyance. I do not directly own a homebuilding company, moving company, or even an Airbnb. Still, I challenged my wife and daughters to pick up on the different types of frictions we encountered and share how they would embrace them to create value if they did own any of those businesses. Each family member shared some pretty interesting frictions they recognized in the process, and I did share their findings along with potential solutions to consider with each organization. This resulted in a better customer service experience and forged a relationship for future business.

Viewing friction from the perspective of pronoyance takes us another step closer to divorcing convention. The average person allows those annoyances to become huge obstacles. They cringe at the thought of complaints and criticism. When we instead begin to see the possibilities and use them to fuel our organization, we find the secret of Premium Friction Fuel.

Simplify Then Multiply

I genuinely appreciate the concept Dan Sullivan, co-founder of Strategic Coach®, shares in his book, *Simplifier-Multiplier Collaboration*. He talks about discovering your strength as a simplifier or a multiplier and then finding someone to work with to bring about bigger and better things through leveraging the art of collaboration. Friction Fuel operates on this same principle. To create Premium Friction Fuel, it's vital to embrace the idea of simplifying and multiplying.

I simplify very fast to see opportunities for large multipliers. My brain naturally processes the 5x5 Principle without much effort. But it's a skill anyone can develop. You look at the surface friction and dig a bit deeper. As you dive, you use fewer words, and with each why, you find more clarity until you get to the exact reason for the friction. It will seem very obscure at face value and may not seem at all connected to your experience. But the moment you arrive at that most basic level—or what I call the authentic level—the real fun begins. That's when I ask myself, "How the heck can I multiply this solution?"

Simplification begins at the highest level. Multiplication originates at the lowest level. When we attempt to multiply before we simplify, we're reacting to a surface problem. This is where bandage and fire extinguisher fixes come into play, and those solutions make you feel like you're dodging the plethora of stuff that keeps coming at you.

Removing the FILM has its roots in simplification and multiplication. By simplifying, you identify the true source of the friction and figure out who it affects. Leveraging the Friction brings the multiplication.

And if simplifying doesn't seem to come naturally to you, Dan Sullivan suggests you find a simplifier to work with.

Likewise, if you've already mastered the concept of simplifying but can't quite grasp multiplying, I concur with Dan when he recommends finding a multiplier to leverage the art of collaboration for exponential growth.

You might be a business owner, the shipping manager, or the one unloading trucks all day. Regardless of where you stand, you have to decide if the immediate problem is just a temporary annoyance or something deeper. As I share with my girls all the time, "Creators don't complain, and complainers don't create." By digging deep to understand what is really going on, you can become a creator and start to see how to resolve the issue. Then you can ask, "Who am I creating value for?" and "How many people am I creating value for?" This awareness is extremely important because one of those people who find value in your innovation may be your next big multiplier.

Every step of the way, you're creating intellectual property. So, recognizing everyone who benefits from your friction-leveraging idea can impact your organization and empower you to not only level up your organization but also evolve your business into something new. All because you stayed aware, created a process to capture friction, simplified it, and then used those seeming obstacles to multiply for your department, division, organization, industry, and the entire planet. At this point, you're already well on your way to the next Friction Fuel Strategy—Monetize Your Experience Divorce the Convention.

Chapter 4

The Secret to Divorcing Convention

THERE'S NOTHING WRONG WITH convention as long as you don't mind average. However, if you've implemented strategies to capture and resolve friction, then deep inside, you know you were made for something bigger. That means it's time to divorce conventional thinking and forge ahead in using the friction to leverage the market.

Eight-year-old me saw friction in the horse sale arena my father and I went to a few times a week. I'd been riding horses since I learned to walk, so I made even the most cantankerous horse look like a gentle giant, and I recognized that kid-friendly horses brought more money at these auctions. Adults who didn't ride thought that since kids could ride horses, they should be able to handle it when they got home as well. Though no one had ever invited young boys to ride the stock at a horse auction before, the owners decided to take a chance on my experience and allow me to alleviate their friction. And each trip through the sale ring garnered me a ten-dollar bill for my skills.

Those sale barns gave me my first taste of what I call "MYEX (Monetize Your Experience) Divorce the Convention." Fortunately, activating this second ingredient of Friction Fuel is easily within reach.

Becoming Aware of Your Uniqueness

Every person on the planet has plenty of experience. Unfortunately, many have a difficult time recognizing its real worth. They have identified with their industry, business, or title for so long that seeing the value their experience brings outside that arena becomes challenging. Time and time again, I have watched entrepreneurs work hard in their companies and build until they reach their pinnacle. I've heard more than one executive tell me, "I'm done with this." And I believe them. They're tired. They've spent years investing their entire being into building their business, and they have nothing left to give. Still, they have a deep, subconscious, emotional attachment. The limbic part of their brain ties this lifelong endeavor to their identity. Sadly, the day after they sell, they're lost. With more money than they've ever seen before in their pocket, they hit the golf course or travel the world, but without purpose, they soon feel displaced and depressed.

When our identity is tied to our business, rather than the mounds of experience we developed during those building years and our authentic expression of how we create value in the world, we flounder. On the other hand, when we embrace the idea that "I am not driven by what I am, I am driven by what I am becoming," our identity turns into an ever-evolving and growing organism—something that is always bigger and better.

One man I worked with operated in an industry that required constant price updates. Over thirty years, he had created extensive spreadsheets and processes to get the job done quickly and efficiently. However, when I talked to him about his uniqueness, he identified as a manufacturer. Because of frictions, he had uncovered in his business, he had developed valuable intellectual property. If someone else in his industry had asked about it, he would have gladly given it away for free, and a couple of times before he realized its worth, he did. By not acknowledging this value creation gold as his own intellectual property, he left money on the table. This seems to be what humans do with things that come easy for them.

Instead of recognizing the value this business owner created by doing his work the way he always did it, he simply chalked their invention up to doing what needed done to yield the returns in the conventional business model.

After we talked, his mindset began to shift. He took his spreadsheets and turned them into a product and service and sold them to the others in his industry—people whose contacts he already had in his phone and CRM. Without realizing it, he had developed a product that didn't hold to the conventions of his industry. He ended up creating a recurring business model that grew much more enterprise value than his legacy business.

One of the greatest assets associated with this discovery is the shift in identity. Within just a few years, this business owner sold his manufacturing company. But by this time, he had already developed a deep, subconscious, emotional association with his new business of creating value. No longer defined by the company he had built, his identity was now tied to his experience and the evolution of his intellectual property—his UVC.

Strategic Coach helps people discover their Unique Ability®—"something you love to do and do best." It "makes you who you are." When you take that Unique Ability and apply it, you now have your Unique Value Contribution.

Discovering your UVC is essential to developing an awareness of your deeper identity to create value, something only you can do. You might call yourself an engineer, but I would argue that you have a UVC you apply to engineering to create a unique outcome. Too many struggle with creating the separation between their job title and their ability to create value.

Yes, it's much easier to share your conventional title at a party or networking event. But how many memorable conventional titles do you recall when you look for someone of the highest value when a friend asks for a referral? By embracing your UVC, you will begin to stand out and help others "refer" your uniqueness. But how do you find this new title to share?

Take the first step by asking, "What are the three to five things only I can do?" Not only in your department or company but in your industry. Even if you know someone who can accomplish something similar, this list will include the things you do in an unconventional way—tasks you can't hand off to someone else. What do others in your organization rely on you for? It's tempting for early-stage entrepreneurs to answer that question with "everything." And if you want to remain in the "early stages" forever, keep doing everything. But honestly, much of the day-to-day work can be passed on to someone else—a person with the UVC to carry out those important tasks. You have a one-of-a-kind process or innovation. It's time to become aware of your rare genius and embrace it.

Be aware—we all run into things that stall us. I know as clearly as anyone how easy it is to get stuck and not take action, and I've studied solutions to this problem. A good friend of mine, Dean Jackson, recently shared an observation he had on the subject. Dean is a savant in marketing and a huge simplifier. He noticed three consistent things keeping people from making forward progress. As always, Dean shared a profound awareness—something I call The 3Ls.

Moving Past the 3Ls of Why Not Now?

Often, we find our momentum stalled, but we can't figure out what happened. We had an awesome idea and shared it with a team. We even used Dan Sullivan's Impact Filter™ to properly communicate the project. This created even more friction, but we've learned how to leverage friction. Why can't we move forward?

After Dean and I talked, I began to understand his concept, and it began to really come into focus. So, I created a tool for myself so that when I find myself stuck, I can leverage Dean's wisdom.

I found the best place to start when my or my team's objective seems to run off into a ditch is to ask why. Building off the 5x5 Principle, I begin with a new why: Why not now? And the answer will continue to track back to one of the 3Ls:

1. **Logic**—You have a mental block. If the reason for the stall is a logic problem, you'll find yourself asking, "What should I or we do? Experience tells me there are times when we have no real clue about WHAT we should do. We find ourselves standing at a crossroads, not knowing exactly what should happen next.

2. **Logistics**—You might have a legitimate shortage of information if you keep saying, "I don't know how to do it." Often, we'll know exactly what the next step should be, but we won't have the skills or processes in place. Simply put, we don't know HOW to create the success projected by the WHAT.

3. **Limbic**—If the lack of an emotional attachment is what holds you back, you'll find yourself asking, "Why does this matter? Why am I doing this anyway?" Let's face it. It happens. We start out excited about a project or an outcome, but for some reason, we lose interest. Without an attachment to the outcome, the project just doesn't have the same meaning.

The limbic factor is usually the biggest obstacle to moving forward. And often, when logic or logistics freeze us, we definitely need to find a WHO. Some frictions will be so large they need more than one person to implement the idea. Discovering the root of your procrastination will allow you to create some Friction Fuel to move past it. You may need to ask a few more whys to truly understand the lack of action. You might need to enlist the help of a coach or a partner to ferret out what you should do. A logistics block might be answered by something as simple as collaborating with someone who does know how to do it. And a limbic block may mean you need to pass your idea on to someone else who has the passion necessary to bring the best outcome.

The most important part of the 3Ls is increasing your awareness of "Why Not Now?" so nothing keeps you from reaching your full potential. Using this simple tool anytime you feel stalled will create an awareness of friction and keep you from running on Regular because the project is overdue, and you're scrambling with your hair on fire.

This concept of The 3Ls has greatly impacted my team at SEEDSPARK since Dean shared it with me. I see them implementing the tool to stay in front of frictions that try to stall some of our most vital projects. I hope it provides you and your team the same value.

Capitalizing on Your Experience

Sadly, many entrepreneurs reach that place of maximum return before they realize they've lost their identity to their business. They don't take time to fully develop their UVC until after they've signed the papers to sell. These creatives then spend years—or a lifetime—in limbo, not sure where to go next.

The answer lies in learning to evolve before life demands it. And if you become aware of your uniqueness at a young age, you may evolve several times before you reach the point of your ultimate UVC.

I evolved from riding horses to training horses, supplying farms to selling mobile phones, consulting on usage analytics and rate plans to educating Blackberries users to creating a software company, and then to founding many other companies and many other interesting endeavors along the way. Every evolution was born out of identifying the friction, divorcing the convention, capitalizing on my previous experience, and leveraging my UVC.

I eventually noticed a few consistencies in each advancement. My natural curiosity allows me to dig deeper into problems than others and see every circumstance as a puzzle with endless possibilities. I have a knack for envisioning a better future for those around me and recognizing value many don't see. Plus, with an intentional focus on the outcome, I can see past convention, which opens the door to endless possibilities. I obviously didn't realize the way I used this identity during my first dozen company-creating evolutions.

For instance, I was barely twenty when I bought the farm store. It started as just a small feed and western clothing shop. And though one of my first lessons was that I'm not crazy about retail, I learned a ton from that experience.

My first friction during those early years was learning to slow down. I've always been a go-go-go individual, and I had to put on the brakes and add inventory more slowly than I liked. Still, I expanded much more quickly than most in the business. I just kept adding products as I saw my Hero Targets' frictions and took action. This resulted in exponential growth and led to Purina Mills asking us to become the first America's Country Store—a new concept that basically embraced the store we had already created. It also netted us a much nicer building.

This link will take you to a photo of the farm supply store.

At that time, I still lived in Pageland, South Carolina, about forty-five minutes away. It didn't take long for my curiosity to wonder how I could capitalize on my commute. To young and single Chad, the wasted time felt like friction. My experience with farms, trailers, and country life helped me see I could pick up shavings from a chicken farm on my way home and dump them on the way to the store the next morning, ready for sale. I had to invest in a dump trailer, but the extra hundred dollars a day I made not only paid for the trailer, it created an expense-free commute.

By embracing your talents—those things no one else could do, you clear the path to a lifetime of adventure. You never have to look at your identity in a conventional manner again. This awareness invites you to MYEX—Divorce the Convention.

Consider your largest competitors. Can any of them do what you do the way you do it? Do they have your experience? Can they do it as well? Probably not. By packaging your UVC, you can turn yourself into a business services company and create the kind of value that allows you to Divorce the Convention and make clients out of your competitors.

Imagine how different it would be if this became the convention—every organization specializing in their own UVC and collaborating with others doing the same. How much better off would we all be, and how much additional value would your Hero Targets receive over today's convention? Watch for the answer to that question in a later chapter.

After I walked through this process with that manufacturer, he recognized how he could Divorce the Convention of being under so much regulation and build enterprise value much faster than his current industry. Selling his company would be lucrative. A manufacturing company is worth about three times its EBITDA (Earnings Before Interest, Taxes, Depreciation, and Amortization). If your business makes a million dollars a year, it's worth about three million.

On the other hand, if you have a recurring services company—something easily created by naming, packaging, messaging, and offering your process—it will be worth about ten to fourteen times EBITDA. Your million-dollar subscription business will be valued at fourteen million. The best part is that if you've developed this UVC to help with friction in a present department or industry, you've already paid for your cost of goods. That manufacturer had been doing it for twenty-five years. Every penny in this next stage of his life would be profit.

Regardless of your business, you have something only you do. And it's something someone else needs—whether in your industry, your city, or a particular department across industries—someone else is experiencing that friction. Your experience has more value than you realize, but in order to capitalize on it, you will have to Divorce the Convention. By executing MYEX—Divorce the Convention, you set yourself up for psychological and financial success. You can redefine your identity, and your life can start running on Premium Friction Fuel. Trust me; it pays much better!

Focusing on Your Hero Target

One pitfall in business is the tendency to use charts and reports to determine your next step instead of focusing on friction trends. "Follow the Money" has become a familiar mantra in business. I recommend a less conventional approach—one I embraced when I had little business experience and no budget for marketing— "Make It Easy for People to Do Business with You."

In the early days of my farm supply store, long before smartphones were the norm, I had communication problems with my delivery guys. To alleviate the friction, I partnered with Nextel to provide phones for my team as well as my clients. Farmers and contractors loved having the ease of communication added to our inventory. When I focused on my Hero Targets and their inability to make money when they had to stop in and pick up a phone or renew their plans on a regular basis, I divided the city into small quadrants and sent service vehicles out like ice cream trucks to deliver and service clients.

This strategy moved the needle for sure in the "Make it easy for People to do Business with You" realm. I simply took the product to them—such an easy fix. I recommend you constantly look for options that let you go to your Hero Targets versus them having to come to you. Sometimes, the biggest competitive advantages are the simplest.

During that period, phone plans changed frequently, and mobile phone usage was exploding. Keeping up with the added complexities of managing company plans to save money became frustrating and time-consuming, and the responsible parties didn't have complete focus on the new rate plans and usage patterns. Since I had first-hand knowledge of the new rate plans each month, it seemed to be a natural fit for me to help those Hero Targets. The other folks in the industry laughed at me when I set up a subscription plan. They didn't think anyone would ever pay someone to review their bill every month. Sadly for them, they were wrong.

For five dollars a month, I took a look at their usage and recommended the best plan. My clients' plans ranged from several dozen to several thousand phones, so adding managed wireless service saved them much more than the monthly fee. By focusing on creating value for my Hero Target, I developed a lucrative recurring business model and quickly learned this was my favorite way to do business.

My friend Dean Jackson says, "Show up at the receiving dock, not the procurement office." What would your product or service look like if your clients received it at their doors like Amazon® packages rather than like a bill collector with his hand out for more money? Each month, my team delivered savings reports and future savings projections to our managed wireless clients. The trust we developed was immeasurable. I can't count the number of referrals it brought.

As the Blackberry began to hit the mainstream, I noticed another friction. The need for IT services was growing, and my Hero Targets were struggling. Small-to-medium-sized businesses can't afford a dedicated Technology Department. To alleviate that friction, I created two companies—one I still own today. C2 Technologies was born to service the needs of my targets. We set up servers with email and cyber security to drive the business growth of our clients. This led to the purchase of three other technology companies as well as a portion of a data center. Every move was driven by Removing the FILM methodology and focusing on Premium Friction Fuel to keep me way out in front of the competition.

Zig Ziglar said it best: "You will get all you want in life if you help enough other people get what they want." Convention concentrates on the bottom line, but it's not about you or your organization. It's not about the industry. The goal is a positive outcome for the Hero Target. When you focus on your Hero Targets and their friction with eyes wide open, you create an environment for natural and rapid growth.

I was still very young when I created that technology company, and the concept of scaling was completely foreign to me; however, because my primary focus was the customer, we built relationships with them, and they turned into lifelong clients. As a bonus, my annual revenue grew in exponential proportions simply because I used my Unique Value Contribution to create value for my Hero Targets.

Chapter 5

Your Unique Value Contribution

E VERY ENTREPRENEUR RUNNING ON Premium Friction Fuel has created processes to resolve problems. Dan Sullivan calls them shortcuts. Most executives think the way they bring in new clients or address new projects is normal. They believe everyone uses their methods. But these HOWs are much more unique than you might think, and they are golden. Every day, I witness small to medium businesses and their entrepreneurs creating intellectual property. Because they don't recognize it as a Unique Value Contribution, they leave money on the table.

Your UVC has the ability to multiply and leverage both your current market and new markets. After you become aware of your new identity that had been masked inside the convention of your industry and recognize the potential for your capability rather than continuing to give it away, it's time for NPMO—name it, package it, message it, and offer it—so you can share your UVC with the planet and get paid for your unique way of creating value.

Name the Baby

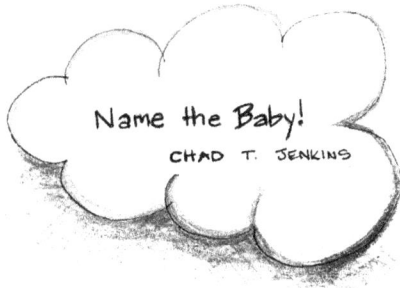

When a collaboration is made to create something NEW, you have to "Name the Baby!"

"Thanks to Miss Lisa Cini for our Name the Baby Graphic."

Even before the infant's birth, parents start picking out names. This book had a title before I wrote the first word. We identify songs, movies, and even our animals by their unique monikers. Yet, when was the last time you gave one of your processes anything more than a simple attribute on your computer? Like a book needs a great cover, and your dog deserves a better name than Brown Dog, your innovation merits a memorable phrase or acronym. I often say, "If you had a baby and I had a baby, and we didn't name them, I'm not sure whose would be whose."

When I discuss UVC with entrepreneurs, they tend to describe the unique value they create with a series of bullet points. This common practice in answering the question, "What makes your company different than the competition?" is wonderful for internal meetings where you want to give your team the inside scoop on everything you do to create a competitive advantage.

I became aware that even those inside my organization can't easily remember each and every bullet point; however, they can remember a name. I told myself, "Heck, if my team can only remember a few points, and they work with this every day, how in the world will our clients remember the special things we do to create value for them?" So I began thinking deeper about this concept of names, and our "Name the Baby" concept and the tools that go with it were born.

The manufacturer I mentioned earlier figured out how to resolve friction within five years of starting his business. His company grew steadily, running on Premium, because he created processes to manage friction. For twenty years, he refined his innovation; however, he never bothered naming it. Which meant he never packaged it, messaged it, or offered it to the world. He missed the opportunity to elevate beyond his industry and reap the rewards for his primary ways of creating value.

Naming your process and finding something catchy that appeals to your Hero Target feels foreign to most people. Entrepreneurs spend their time brainstorming the next big idea, so taking time to explore the perfect hook slows them down. That's why I designed a simple tool for naming your baby. Now, when I say simple, I don't want you to think it's easy. It will take a bit of time and effort. But the steps are simple.

To get the perfect name, we need to describe our Hero Target as well as our Hero Target's Hero Target in detail. Consider the things that move them, as well as their values and struggles. Most people act out of fear and greed, so our job is to speak to the emotional seat of that person we want to be a hero to. On a whiteboard, make a list of the ways your Hero Target would describe the outcome or the way they feel when you do your very best work. What do they experience? What emotions does your highest level of effort evoke? Write each word on the left side of the board, one per line. As you go back over the list, say each word out loud and mimic your Hero Targets as you speak.

Next, use the middle of the board to give each word a grade from one to five. If you can feel the spoken word in the limbic part of your brain right above your ear, give that word a number five. If you don't, it gets a one. If you sense a little pull, you could give it a three or four. No matter how great the word sounds logically, you're looking for something that hits you emotionally.

After you've graded each word, transfer all the fours and fives to the right side of the board and begin to trim them. Remove letters from each word like you're cutting fat from a steak. Do this with each one, remembering to maintain the integrity of the word. Then, try to stick two of them together and see if it makes sense. It's imperative to retain the interpretation and the feeling of the word. Keep trimming and merging until you find the word that lights up that emotional part of your brain.

Next, go register that domain and visit Instant IP™ (InstantIP. app) to protect your newly named property via Blockchain. You just created intellectual property with that new word; it belongs to you. Instant IP™ provides an immediate first step to prove your ownership with an immutable time-stamped smart contract. No one on the planet can claim origin. You were there first, and you have a smart contract to prove it.

When your Hero Target hears your new process name, they won't need a tagline or copy to convince them to listen because it causes them to lean in. They want that outcome. Just the sound of it makes them want to know more. By naming with intentionality, you touch their emotional side, and you win in the sea of white noise and endless proposals full of bullet points. It is especially powerful with decision-makers when you combine a guarantee with it. Plus, giving your process or service a unique identity empowers your Hero Targets to become ambassadors or part-time salespeople for you. They can more easily embrace it if they can call it by name—especially when they begin to share it with other prospects.

And now that it's named, it's time to prepare it to meet the world.

```
┌─────────────────────┐
│                     │
│      Premium        │
│      Friction       │
│                     │
└─────────────────────┘
           │
           ▼
┌─────────────────────┐
│                     │
│      Naming,        │
│   Packaging, &      │
│     Messaging       │
│                     │
└─────────────────────┘
           │
           ▼
┌─────────────────────┐
│                     │
│      Offering       │
│                     │
└─────────────────────┘
```

Package It Pretty

"Don't judge a book by its cover" has been a cliché for decades. Despite hearing the phrase over and over, we still make snap judgments on presentation and wrapping paper. Moreover, we don't want to have to jump through half a dozen hoops or take a college class to purchase and use the latest gadgets or systems. User-friendly has turned into more than a buzzword.

So, after you've named your innovation, you have to decide how you will make it available to the public. Will it be a one-time purchase or a subscription? You already described your perfect client when you named the baby. Now you have to decide what kind of package will make it most convenient for your Hero Target to get their hands on your system? Ease of acquisition should be your number one priority as you think about presenting your Unique Value Contribution to the world.

Sometimes your packaging will include an entirely new company name—especially if you plan to turn competitors into clients. Over the last twenty-five years, friction solutions have been the source for many of the businesses I've started. Seldom will you identify friction unique to your business. So, you'll want to package your Friction Fuel in such a way that others in your industry see your solution to their friction as well.

Communicate Your Message

The only way to truly help your Hero Target is to get your UVC into their hands. So, the next step is asking, "How will I communicate awareness for the need I solved?" Some will create a landing page or a website, and many times you'll find a starter database in your phone because your vendors and those in your industry—people you come in contact with on a regular basis—need your solution or know businesses that need it.

Most of the businesses I started came about because I love solving friction for my Hero Targets. This means I had built-in clients. Because they were already working with me in one area, they felt comfortable working with my new companies as I added them. For instance, those who used my phone service were my first clients when I started creating apps for their Blackberries. When I added the software solutions company, these clients were my first contacts. Plus, they're always ready and anxious to help me spread the word. Keeping your Hero Targets as the focus of your message will help mold your communication.

Offer Your Innovation

After you've decided the best way to Message your product or service, it's time to begin to offer your revolutionary idea to the world. It's vital to remember that the most successful endeavors don't try to do it alone.

This means, when you're ready to share your innovation with those who need it, you'll start with the people who know and trust you and also do business with your Hero Target. Collaborating with this audience is the fastest way to scale with your new product or service. I'll get into the four types of collaboration in the next chapter; however, you can start making your list of potential partnerships now. How much of your profit are you willing to share with those who "refer" your innovation?

Your Unique Value Contribution has more worth than you might realize. By recognizing it as the path to Premium Friction Fuel and then Naming, Packaging, Messaging, and Offering it, you can increase your profitability while you make your Hero Target's life a little easier.

Collaboration Growth Catalyst—Using Your UVC to Create Your Next UVC

After you've developed tremendous clarity around your UVC, it's time to take it to the next level. By leveraging the art of collaboration with others who share your mindset, you can unlock exponential growth and value creation. This is a glimpse into the work and process we use with our SEEDSPARK Growth Partners all over the world.

1. Gather your team and put your UVC at the top of a whiteboard.
2. Create three columns—one for your competitors, one for vendors, and a third for your clients.

3. Take some time to stare at the board.

4. Evaluate each of these companies against your UVC.

5. Keep staring until you begin to see ways you and the other companies on your chart can leverage each other to create new UVCs.

6. Next, on the bottom of the board, write the value creation you see and circle the companies you could work with to bring your new UVC to fruition.

7. After you've written a few new ideas on your board, give each a ranking of one to five. Ones offer little impact to your hero target. Fives bring a sizable shift and greater outcome to your hero target.

8. Finally, rank each idea by effort required on your part. Five for little effort and one being a heavy lift.

9. Add the numbers associated with each idea, and for the three with the highest score, list your first three action steps to bring it to reality, and then name the baby.

By continually gathering to stare at the whiteboard, we can repeat the process indefinitely to come up with new collaborators and value creations. Over time, this can result in a new suite of products and services to directly add value to your Hero Targets. One of the best things about using this tool is that you can begin using this today. You don't have to go to another company, expand a department, or even spin a new website to create value for your Hero

Targets. If you're willing to practice this simple exercise, you can leverage the art of collaboration today. And if you implement this strategy, you should hold on tight! You're about to grow aggressively.

Chapter 6

Become a Premium Fuel Refinery Through Collaboration

F ROM REGULAR TO PREMIUM Friction Fuel, most companies run horizontally. Premium takes on that aggressive path; however, it's still horizontal. All entrepreneurs start with the logic of horizontal growth. It's just easier to carry out. Vertical growth can seem abstract until you fully understand it. In fact, only the most mature, those who've abandoned the blinders that keep them focused on their own industry and conventional thinking, can truly expand vertically.

Horizontal Growth

Imagine a long road in front of your business with a mailbox at the end of the driveway. This path represents your Hero Target's journey. When one of them engages with your business it's as if they stopped at your mailbox. Everyone knows yours won't be the only mailbox they stop at. Each customer came from somewhere, and they'll be interacting with another business after they leave you.

When entrepreneurs begin, they're pretty good at looking up and down the road. Where did your Hero Target come from, and with what other projects or services did they engage? We look at what they needed at each place they stopped as well as how the mailboxes they visit after leaving ours will serve them. Businesses running on Plus or Premium Friction Fuel look left and right to see the other people or places who value their Hero Target.

Acknowledging The Obstacle is the Way means we become a Friction Fuel Refinery. We've developed the processes, named it, packaged it, and more. And now it's time for the next principle: If the obstacle is the way, collaboration is the way through[IP].

Every person on the planet collaborates on a regular basis. Any time you combine two or more people, places, or things to create value, you have collaborated. You plus time plus a spreadsheet is collaboration. Believe it or not, when you get in your car and travel to a desired destination, you collaborate with the car, the road, and perhaps a GPS. The obstacle creates a way—a reason to move forward. Collaboration takes you through to success.

Horizontal growth comes from looking forward and backward down the road to discover how you can collaborate. I named the two most basic forms—Partner Collaborations[IP] (PCB) and Referral Collaborations[IP] (RCB).

A PCB is easy to spot. Think about your top five clients. You probably know them by their first name, and I assume the road has not been completely smooth during your relationship. I expect you've had rough patches where you came together, discussed issues, and worked together to come up with a solution. Furthermore, I am confident this solution provided value, confirmed by the fact these clients continue to pay you, renew agreements, and send referrals. That is the exact definition of a Partner Collaboration.

Now that you're aware of ways to alleviate friction for your top five clients, you may consider Naming the Baby and extending the service to all your clients. Your clients will be impressed when they realize you understand the road won't always be smooth but you take them so seriously you're willing to embrace the potholes and work in collaboration with those you serve to find a way to travel on smooth pavement together.

Let's face it, we've all changed vendors before. It's expensive and uncomfortable. Just to consider evolving your approach to include Partner Collaborations will be viewed favorably by your current and prospective Hero Targets.

Referral Collaboration happens when two or more parties agree to share each other's products or services to realize an expanded reach and a bigger customer base. Generally, you'll see RCB between two businesses in adjacent industries. For instance, a tax consultant might work closely with a wealth management advisor. Or a wholesale manufacturer might develop a referral relationship with one of their top Hero Targets recommending the retail manufacturer when a customer who doesn't qualify for wholesale purchases calls. The two entities remain entirely separate, and little, if any, money exchanges hands. In fact, I believe the exchange of funds tends to shorten the life of the Referral Collaboration. It's vital to remember to keep your focus on your Hero Targets for value creation. If you commit to this strategy, your phone will ring, and it will ring for the right reasons.

Referral Collaboration may not always include one-to-one referrals. You might send ten customers for every one referred to you; however, the value you provide your Hero Targets brings trust and gratitude which translates to loyalty. Loyal customers become clients, and when you add a new product or service, they'll want to do business with you on that level as well.

RCB provides value for the Hero Target because they've already developed a relationship with one of the referral collaborators. This lets them feel more comfortable working with that entrepreneur's recommendations. They know the referral has been closely vetted because neither collaborator can afford to have their name associated with someone who underproduces.

Look for these partnerships to extend down the road both ways to reach a capacity you never imagined. I experienced massive horizontal growth at the farm store through collaboration. Every PCB I introduced alleviated my Hero Target's friction. The trailer supplier I partnered with resolved friction. The banks I collaborated with provided loans for my Hero Target who liked instant gratification and didn't mind living beyond their means. They also taught me about financing and interest rates and gave me my first taste of recurring revenue. I learned that retailers often add a point or two to the interest to compensate them for their trouble. I quickly learned to enjoy recurring revenue.

Joint Venture Collaboration

Joint Venture Collaboration (JCB) is one of my favorite kinds of horizontal partnerships. JCB occurs when two or more parties produce a potentially improved value proposition. The collaboration might enhance an existing product or service, or it may lead to an entirely new endeavor.

The first step to this collaboration is making a list of those vendors who see your clients just before and just after you. Then you can meet with them to discuss the current value you each bring to your Hero Target as well as potential outcomes and value creation. After establishing a meaningful combined UVC, you pay the other company for their product or service and pass it along to your Hero Target.

For example, many years ago when a woman did her daily shopping, she stopped at the general store for sundries, then bought a loaf of bread from the baker and a roast from the butcher. On the way home, she stopped at the mill and the chicken farm to buy flour and eggs; and if she had no cow, her milk, cheese, and butter had been delivered to her doorstep before the children woke.

At some point, the general store owner realized he could save his Hero Target a few minutes every day by partnering with the baker. He purchased bread and baked goods for a few cents less than he sold it to the woman at the baker's retail price. The store owner made a few cents, and the baker didn't lose any money because he didn't need a store front anymore. The baker became a vendor, freeing him to bake and provide even more goodness for his Hero Target.

Soon, the dairy realized they could save time and money if they gave the storekeeper a few cents on each bottle of milk and bowl of butter rather than take it door to door every morning. Before you know it, a grocery store had bloomed. No longer were the storekeeper's vendors all in big cities many miles away. More and more local specialists partnered with the general store to carry their goods, benefiting the Hero Target as well as each collaborator.

Many times, it's easier for you to see the potential value the person behind and in front of you can create than it is to see your own. We humans are much better critics than we are developers. By stepping outside yourself and into your Hero Targets' shoes, you will be able to more effectively see how your neighbors can serve those people who stop at your mailbox. With outside-of-the-box thinking, you can find ways to bundle your services or help solve friction for your Hero Targets in other businesses—turning your competitors into clients. All the while creating value for your Hero Targets.

In Joint Ventures, both parties profit, either through increased margins, value, or viability, and compensation is split based on each party's contribution to the new outcome. But more important than the benefits to the partners is the value and convenience you can bring to your Hero Target by always providing them with the highest quality and performance.

You can take Joint Ventures one step further and *Just Add a Zero* by applying the split the outcome approach. Collaborators that enter these Joint Ventures share the risk of an unknown profit; however, both also reap the benefits of a larger-than-expected payout. For example, at fifteen, I mowed grass-covered lots all around Charlotte for an expanding bank chain. Eventually, the number grew too big for me to handle alone. I had plenty of trucks, tractors, trailers, and bush hogs available from the farm. I just needed bodies. Fortunately, I had a few friends who also knew how to drive tractors and operate bush hogs, so I proposed they partner with me. They would do the work, and after I got paid, I would give them a percentage. Since I didn't have upfront cash, I needed them to be more than hourly employees who got paid on a promised payday every week. By collaborating with them on a split the outcome basis, when I got paid, they got paid. And they made a lot more than others that engaged in the traditional hourly wage principle—trading time for money with no upside.

This form of collaboration can work well for any company. Because all partners have a stake in the outcome, everyone works toward the same goal. Often, the payout is substantially more than either party originally expected. In my farm supply days, one gentleman approached me about upgrading the interior of horse trailers so they could be used as camping trailers. He wanted $22,000 to create the new interior. I suggested he reinvent just one horse trailer, I would sell it on my lot, and we could split the profit. By splitting the outcome, he netted an extra $6,000 and created a mutually beneficial trust relationship that lasted until I exited the business.

Using the House's Money

One creative way to split the outcome is what I call "Using the House's Money." Everyone loves winning that first bet in Vegas—especially when you can put your original money back in your pocket and use the gain to take the next risk. This makes it impossible to lose, you're simply taking chances on the excess. Split the outcome has this same potential especially when you starting playing with future money.

Often, small businesses leave money on the table when they don't capitalize on their future earnings. We all have capacity that's already paid for. We pay for utilities whether the building is open or not. Our trucks often move in the direction of the money. What if we used that mindset I had when I hauled shavings?

In the simplest realm, using the house's money is owning a building that's empty on Tuesday evening. You rent it to an event coordinator with the understanding you will be paid based on the number of tickets sold after the concert. You could easily make ten percent more than if you merely rented it for your base fee. And you'll net one hundred percent more than if it sat empty on that evening.

Vertical Growth

While JCB is generally horizontal growth—you look for collaborators who don't work in your industry—it can work to produce vertical growth as well.

Vertical growth includes a few specific prerequisites. Those who scale upward have zeroed in on their Hero Target. They have defined that avatar perfectly so they can foresee friction and identify needs before they arise. These entrepreneurs feel extremely comfortable in their own skin. They have to because vertical growth often means working with businesses that conventional thinking calls "the competition." Epictetus, a stoic philosopher said, "Wealth consists not in having great possessions, but in having few wants." This describes the business person ready for vertical growth. People with a scarcity mindset have a difficult time collaborating vertically.

Vertical Growth is Super Premium Friction Fuel. You might even call it Rocket Fuel. In order to grow vertically, you have to look for those in your industry who have perform at a higher level than you as well as those who do what you do at a lesser level. You need companies who share your work ethic and values who also have different specializations and client lists.

Let's say you own a residential plumbing business that serves a town of fifty to one hundred thousand people. Your company specializes in outdoor plumbing needs. Your crew gets calls for in-the-wall plumbing and finishing work from time to time, but your team crushes outdoor projects. Another contactor near you specializes in getting the pipes in the walls and fixing them when they break. They have to rent equipment if they get an outdoor job, and it takes them twice as long as it takes you. A third company takes care of boilers. They have the licenses necessary to do that work, but you've talked to their team, and you know they end up with outdoor jobs and traditional plumbing even though it slows them down miserably.

What would happen if you met the guys who owned the second and third company for coffee and had a conversation? "Hey, I've got this crazy idea. What if your companies and mine collaborated? We could come up with a joint name and change the signs on our trucks to say 'Joey's Plumbing powered by our Joint Name' and 'Jakes Plumbing powered by . . .' and 'Johnnie's Plumbing powered by . . .'. I think we could corner the plumbing market in the metro area." With each company focusing on what they do best, you can rest assured your partnership will always get five-star reviews. You save money and time because everyone is working more efficiently, your crews are all happier because they get to do what they do best, and each company shares in the profit. You might grow so big you have to bring in a couple other plumbers from your area to handle the overflow. Every time you add a specialist, you shrink your competition, because anyone who is any good is now your collaborator. And best of all, the Hero Target enjoys a more robust product or service and starts telling his friends to only use businesses powered by your new company.

Growth Collaboration

Okay, by now, you're likely ready to remove all your competition. I believe the most exciting vertical growth comes through Growth Collaboration[IP] (GCB). This high-level partnership happens when two or more unrelated parties combine their unique value contributions to create a brand-new enhanced value for their mutual Hero Target. With the Hero Target always at the center of our thinking, we save our clients time, energy, and money with our collaboration. Much like the plumbers in our JCB, the hero target benefits by getting the best of everyone involved. But in Growth Collaboration, the products and services provided by the two or three companies are generally completely different. However, the Hero Target deals only with one contact. She has only one contract to sign. As a bonus, all vendors involved double their sales team, marketing dollars, trust relationships, and online presence. Can you see the bigger picture here?

In a GCB, your combined vision and creativity create so much mutual value that a handshake is enough to cement the deal. The innovation will also be so big it will need a name and a package that both sales teams can offer to their respective Hero Targets. Growth Collaboration has the added benefit of the ability to be sustained for twenty-five or more years.

Collaboration will definitely keep you running on Premium Friction Fuel and can be key in taking you past the 3Ls; however, I've discovered most entrepreneurs need some extra training and network opportunities to kick their organization into high gear.

You might be able to work through these factors and ferret out what's behind your stalled momentum on your own. But I am passionate about helping entrepreneurs go faster and further with Friction Fuel. Feel free to take every word you've read and self-implement; however, if you want some personalized assistance to get the best mileage imaginable, I've got good news.

Part Three: CoLAB

Chapter 7

The Collaboration Station

AFTER DEVELOPING SOMETHING NEW in your space and packaging your awesome UVC, it's time to find the person—the WHO—to execute your idea. Until recently, each time I discovered a new form of Premium Friction Fuel, I simply formed a new LLC. This means I developed new logos, websites, accounting systems, HR policies, procedures, leases, and equipment and had to hire a bunch of people.

Over the last few years, I've changed my process. After being fortunate enough to be invited to join Strategic Coach and working with Julia Waller to identify my own Unique Ability and ultimately define my own UVC, I've developed a new collaboration strategy that leverages my Unique Value Contribution. (I strongly suggest every entrepreneur become involved with Strategic Coach—StrategicCoach.com)

This revelation has helped me use the highest form of Premium Friction Fuel to develop a network of global entrepreneur collaborators. Although the businesses I created in the past nearly always included collaborations, today, I simply pass off my packaged energy to the best fit in my network. I partner with them in a split the outcome JVC. Long gone are the days when I take the long road to setting up a completely new company. Leveraging the art of collaboration has enabled me to grow myself and others exponentially faster than in my first twenty-five years of business.

I've been in the collaboration business since I was eight and rode that first horse into the sales arena. Today, I enjoy traveling the planet, meeting entrepreneurs, and hearing their stories to help identify Premium Frictions for them. I enjoy learning more about their Unique Value Contributions. Introducing entrepreneurs with a growth mindset to one another and watching them form partnerships fulfills my passion. We call them Growth Partners at SEEDSPARK.

You could put up solar panels or build a refinery to produce energy for your car. However, most people think it's much easier to pull into a gas station or employ someone else to install their recharging station. Similarly, anyone can implement the ideas and tools of Friction Fuel or enter a collaboration and begin to benefit much faster. Collaborating with the right WHO to shorten the runway to success is a proven growth catalyst. I am living proof.

To get started, I invite you to go to SEEDSPARK.com and register for one of our Friction Fuel Forums. You'll get a taste of the way we identify Premium Friction and put collaboration to work. And for those seeking to run on Plus to Premium Friction Fuel, SEEDSPARK has launched a series of ways for you to increase your level of collaboration.

Collab Development Kit

SEEDSPARK has created a tool to help entrepreneurs unlock growth by leveraging what Dean Jackson identifies as a formula for Success—Vision, Capabilities, and Reach (VCR). I embraced the "Vision + Capabilities x Reach = Success" formula and its simplicity to help entrepreneurs identify ways to grow outside the current conventions. This strategy helps them identify obstacles and map out potential opportunities for collaboration. It also integrates the Strategic Coach framework of "Make it up, make it real, make it recur" to make the process more accessible and actionable.

To put the VCR tool into action, we start again by creating three columns on a whiteboard. This time, in the first column, we unpack our VCR.

1. **Vision**: What unique connections between people, places, and things do you naturally see, and how could they create new opportunities? What do you see that no one else does?

2. **Capability:** What unique capabilities do you have that you have not yet named, packaged, messaged, and offered that would offer significant value if you did? What do you do better than others? It may not

be all your products and services but think about which ones you excel in. Which could you consider leveraging in collaboration with others for exponential growth or have the most confidence in producing the outcome?

3. **Reach:** Who are the key people, groups, or associations that trust you and amplify your influence? No matter how small or large your stage, every entrepreneur has reach—those who trust you and follow your lead.

In the middle column, identify obstacles using the Friction Fuel Formula. What gaps do you see in your VCR?

1. What vision gap prevents you from achieving your full growth potential? Do you struggle to Make it Up—to imagine a bigger potential?

2. What capability gaps keep you from scaling? In what ways do you find it difficult to Make it Real—turn your vision into action?

3. What gaps do you have in your relationships or realm of influence that keep you from reaching the next level? Why do you struggle to Make it Recur—to sustain and scale growth?

In the right column, map your collaborations.

1. Vision: Who has a complementary vision that can help unlock new opportunities? Think about those you know or organizations like Strategic Coach or SEEDSPARK.

2. Capability: Who possesses the skills and resources to fill your gaps? Consider the obvious and the not-so-obvious. Remember the plumber collaboration example? Competitors are an untapped source of collaboration that can produce scale and capabilities.

3. Reach: Whose influence or network can help you overcome obstacles and reach your full growth potential? This list should include other entrepreneurs, associations, and even adjacent industries. Each person you connect with can increase your reach. One partner with ten connections adds that number to your reach. But what happens when you look for influencers with a connection-to-reach ratio of 1:100, 1:1,000, 1:10,000, or more? Always remember: someone has every one of your Hero Targets in their CRM. They might even have their credit card number on file. The holdup is you and your willingness to collaborate.

By exploring these questions, you set yourself up for meaningful collaborations that can scale your business and provide value to your Hero Target. To help you get started, download an example and one of our tools at SEEDSPARK.com/Download-icvcr/.

Growth Academy

Entrepreneurs who have a hard time divorcing convention love SEEDSPARK Growth Academy. In the fast-paced world of entrepreneurship, tried-and-true methods don't have enough fuel to propel you to greatness. Growth Academy curriculum challenges traditional and best-practices thinking and feeds the entrepreneur's relentless quest for success. We have developed this as an extension of our CoLAB platform to provide access not only to our own value creation concepts and tools like Remove the Film[IP], Just Add A Zero[IP], and Why Not Now[IP], as well as many others, but also to provide access to real-world solutions created by our Global Growth Partners. We recognize that entrepreneurs in all types of industries have developed real intellectual property shortcuts, but often, they never impact others. The SEEDSPARK Academy found on the CoLAB app will give you access to these innovations. The app provides exclusive tools and systems to entrepreneurs looking for an edge. Plus, it serves as an outlet to monetize the entrepreneur's UVC.

As a Growth Partner, you have the ability to share and monetize your secret sauce via SEEDSPARK Academy to empower others around the world. And, just like all revenue generated by the SEEDSPARK Growth community, this opportunity carries the 90/10 split with the same portion feeding back into SEEDSPARK INFINITIS and the partners.

This strategic learning helps business leaders who are tired of the status quo Remove the FILM and teaches them how to turn competition into collaboration. Growth Academy aims to help entrepreneurs dive deeper into the three types of Friction Fuel and identify which levels exist in their organization. This learning environment is the gateway to unlocking unconventional strategies and insights that set our partners apart from the competition. It helps them break free from the ordinary and explore new horizons. Every Academy graduate has the potential to become a Friction Fuel Refinery, constantly harnessing the friction and turning it into energy before Regular Fuel slows down their business and clogs the wheels.

CoLAB

 CoLAB

The CoLAB by SEEDSPARK is where growth-minded entrepreneurs find their WHO—those key collaborators to make their 10X vision a reality. We designed this Global WHO finder to help you identify and connect with the right entrepreneurs to collaborate for exponential outcomes far beyond what you could achieve alone.

The fuel for the CoLAB came from a friction I personally experienced—a friction I saw many growth-minded entrepreneurs struggle with. Every day, new ideas surface in the minds of entrepreneurs, but bringing those ideas to life often requires more than just hard work. It requires a special WHO. Long before I fully understood the power of collaboration, I leveraged it in my entrepreneurial journey. Collaboration has always been the rocket that propelled me further.

After reading *Who Not How*® by Dan Sullivan and Dr. Ben Hardy, based on the concept created by my friend Dean

Jackson, I coined a phrase that made this idea even more practical for entrepreneurs: Nothing New Without a WHO[IP]. I also refined my own definition of WHO and turned it into an acronym to make it memorable for me and other entrepreneurs: **W**ith the **H**elp of **O**thers[IP]. It became clear to me that every great thing I've accomplished happened because of a WHO.

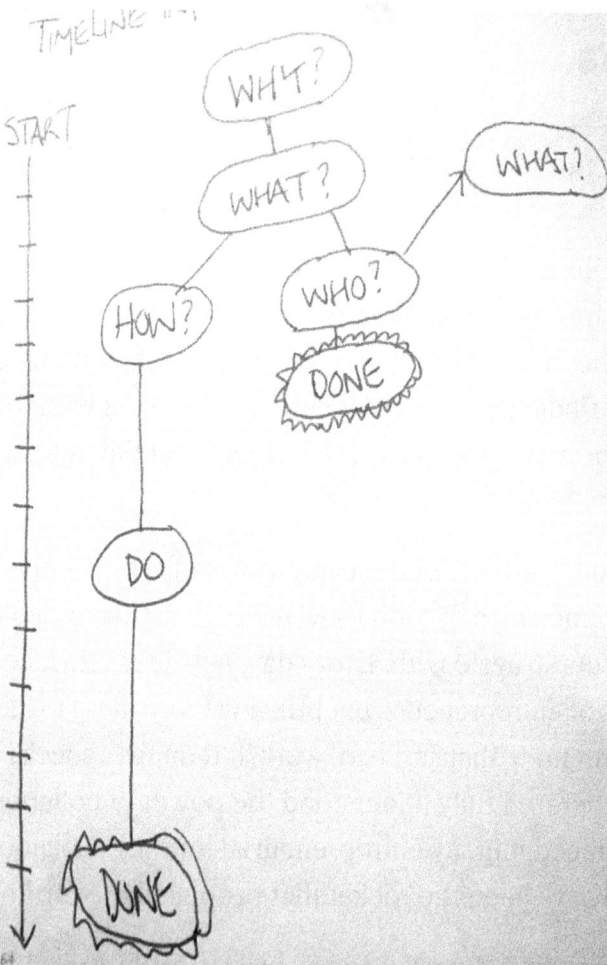

Now, each time I list all the awesome things required to bring my vision to life, I always add a WHO column. Looking back, only "With the Help of Others" have I been able to create anything of value.

As I applied my UVC to this realization, the idea of making this impact even bigger hit me: Why not create a Global **WHO** finder?

So, SEEDSPARK created the world's first Global WHO finder—the SEEDSPARK CoLAB.

Our mission is to empower growth-minded entrepreneurs across the globe to find each other, fostering collaborations that create new and unique value in the world at a scale never seen before. Inside the CoLAB app and platform, entrepreneurs can share insights, explore ongoing discussions about value creation, and collaborate with others from around the world.

SEEDSPARK Academy, part of the CoLAB app, solves yet another friction and provides a 10X opportunity. This is where you'll find our proprietary methods, like Name the Baby (your UVC), which make it easier to identify the right WHO to help you achieve your big vision. We guide you to defy conventional paths and discover the unique value only you can offer.

But SEEDSPARK Academy is bigger than my ideas. The app allows you to access tools created by entrepreneurs all over the world. Prior to the Academy, these innovations sat in spreadsheets on entrepreneurs' hard drives. The only people who used them were the entrepreneurs who created them. Now, with the CoLAB and SEEDSPARK Academy, these entrepreneurs share their "Babies," and users gain access to learning tools and resources, not just from me but from every entrepreneur in the community.

The CoLAB WHO finder also incorporates AI to help curate WHOs based on your needs, connecting you with collaborators whose unique value aligns with your goals. Think of it as LinkedIn®, but exclusively for entrepreneurs focused on growth and collaboration.

One golden rule defines the CoLAB: No selling. Each entrepreneur gives away their best consulting for free. Why? Because when you give without holding back, as if the other person's business were your own, something magical happens. Authenticity breeds trust. Transparency—the good, the bad, and the ugly—emerges. This kind of trust greatly improves the probability of success.

Make no mistake, the CoLAB will drive more business than anything we've seen before. But here's the key difference: It's about collaboration, not transaction. It's not a vendor and buyer exchange. It's about building something together.

Though the best ideas are offered freely, we know most people will need help to bring those ideas to life. While we don't encourage buying and selling, we do promote split the outcome collaboration. SEEDSPARK encourages everyone to ask for help, and after someone makes the ask, both sides are free to engage and create outcomes that align with their visions. To make collaboration even more effective, I recommend applying my concept of Future Money[IP] to truly co-create results.

Why does this matter so much? I'm glad you asked.

Since joining Strategic Coach and focusing on my Unique Ability to ultimately find and name my own UVC, I've realized something important. The reason so many entrepreneurs were open to answering my questions and considering my suggestions for growth wasn't because I had any stake in their business. At the time, I wasn't directly involved in marketing, compensation plan development, logistics management, messaging, or anything else. I simply noticed friction and suggested possible solutions and WHOs. I genuinely wanted to help—to share what I saw as opportunities to create bigger outcomes for them.

After recognizing friction in the bigger market, I saw a way to create real value for many entrepreneurs. Then, I went on to create businesses to provide that value. But I only did this after collaborating with those I served. Those conversations, built on authentic collaboration, have shaped everything I've become. I owe everything to each client who has trusted me—thank you.

This authenticity and willingness to collaborate are the foundations of what we're building with SEEDSPARK's CoLAB and our Growth Partners. So, if you're an entrepreneur who wakes up at night with a 100X idea, or if you want to be part of a community of WHOs to support you in making your vision real, I invite you to explore the SEEDSPARK CoLAB. Join us. You'll find you're not alone; there are many of us ready to share our next big idea, and the CoLAB is where we hang out. We would love to meet you and create something special together. You'll find the app at SEEDSPARK.com/CoLAB or this QR code.

Growth Partners

SEEDSPARK Growth Partners is a movement for growth-minded entrepreneurs from around the world. Our proprietary model of splitting the outcome for each Growth Partner fosters collaborations that provide a catalyst for exponential growth. And best of all—everyone wins. Business collaboration is the key to unlocking unprecedented success and transcending convention of growth in any industry. While individual companies have their strengths, the synergy between businesses creates transformative results.

Our unique concept revolves around forming a true partnership with a company where we collaboratively develop an evolving comprehensive growth mindset plan. This works just as you might expect—by forming collaborations with other growth-minded entrepreneurs who work hand in hand, leveraging each others' UVCs to bring to reality the vision of exponential growth while participating in the outcome. Every Growth Partner is incentivized to bring their best UVC and leverage all aspects of collaboration to defy the growth trajectories, even the fastest growing in their industry experience.

We built the Growth Partners approach on global collaboration and split the outcome ideals. I work with men and women who've built successful businesses ready to scale. They bring the business; I bring my vision and collaboration experience. Whatever amount the value of their business grows while we're working together, they keep ninety percent; SEEDSPARK receives ten. Of this ten percent, seventy percent flows back into the Growth Partner community for their contribution in helping the collaborator reach his or her full potential in their organization. The rest of SEEDSPARK's ten percent goes into SEEDSPARK INFINITUS, a non-profit owned by the Growth Partners. This organization funds the education of SEEDSPARK Academy to develop tomorrow's global entrepreneurs as well as new organizations for aspiring business owners. Growth Partners becomes a win, win, win for everyone involved because together, we can achieve remarkable success.

I believe these Growth Partners can achieve the same kind of success that Ford, Carnegie, and Firestone achieved when working as a team. They said when they got together, they felt as if there was a third mind in the room. Though they didn't call it as such, these men experienced neural entrainment. This happens when you get so aligned with another person that your pulses begin to beat together, and your eyes dilate at the same rate. You become connected at a higher level than verbal and physical, and you feel in sync. I call this Third Mind Innovation[IP] (TMI). TMI provides combined wisdom and unexplainable creativity.

When I reach a TMI plane with another person, everything begins to move very quickly. I can speak fewer words to explain my concepts, and we can fluidly expand our thoughts because it's as if we're on the same wavelength. Because we're like-minded—constantly finding ways to improve for our Hero Target and growing ourselves as much as our businesses—Growth Partners has the potential to reach this level of Third Mind thinking. I feel privileged to witness this happening every day in this group.

It's also these Growth Partners I turn to when I see the path to a new form of Friction Fuel. With such a tremendous variety of business types, one of them is bound to be a perfect fit for my idea. My Vision plus their Capability times another's REACH builds our framework for split the outcome collaboration.

SEEDSPARK Growth Initiative

One of the greatest advantages of becoming involved in a SEEDSPARK program is the frequency of networking and growth opportunities with other growth-minded entrepreneurs from around the world. This brings immediate Reach to each one that joins, a friction I witnessed and experienced in my own journey and love to resolve for other entrepreneurs. When I started, I was so focused on my local market that I had no idea how many opportunities could be produced by knowing others like me around the globe. If you feel alone or like an outsider due to your unwavering commitment to growth or find yourself looking for engaging conversation with people who push you to be better while others seem to be content and center their talk around sports, know that a multitude of us exist, and SEEDSPARK can give you access to your tribe. Just think what could happen if you were surrounded by entrepreneurs just like you, all incentivized to help each other grow.

SEEDSPARK Growth Initiative is also unique in the way it meets. Many other growth initiatives meet quarterly or perhaps less frequently. When you leave the conference, you feel like your head is about to explode. You have so much valuable information you aren't sure how to unpack it all. Soon, the buoyancy of the experience begins to deflate, and it becomes the monkey on your back. When the next event comes around, you discover you've implemented very little.

SEEDSPARK Friction Forums meet bi-monthly and have a maximum occupancy. We often have a panel of experts as well as breakout rooms. This gives everyone in the group an opportunity to ask questions, share, and develop.

In the off weeks, Growth Partners have an opportunity to meet with my Growth Architects—advanced members of the Growth Partners program who have agreed to Shepherd newer entrepreneurs through this journey of leveraging collaborations and SEEDSPARK's value creation tools and concepts. Not only does this keep the juices stirring in the minds of these growing business owners, but it also allows SEEDSPARK's top-level partners to give back—something I feel is every bit as valuable as being in the learning seat. Plus, they're incentivized because when I split the outcome with the person they mentor, they also get a percentage.

By having the potential to meet weekly, either in a net-working atmosphere with one of the SEEDSPARK team or in a Friction Forum with successful entrepreneurs from around the world, participants have an opportunity to revisit, reevaluate, and find WHOs to help collaborate with their plan more often. Bringing ideas to the forefront and creating concrete action steps at tighter and more regular intervals propels their plans forward.

I enjoy creating this connective tissue between growth-minded entrepreneurs. I call it my mycelium. Like the root system of a mushroom bed, these entrepreneurs feed each other and grow together to create something healthier, bigger, better, and more profitable than they can imagine.

Helping others Identify Friction and find collaborations so entrepreneurs can defy conventional growth trajectories has become my highest level of Friction Fuel. It drives me and makes me a better business owner, husband, and father, which also feeds my identity. Working as a unit, these partners and I can Add Zeros and Remove the FILM. We innovate together and grow together. And all the while, we have fun keeping our businesses running on Premium.

About the Author

Chad's zeal to understand how businesses work allows him to immediately understand and identify invisible opportunities in "the way we have always done it."

When Chad couples his three foundational elements—Apply the FILM, Just Add a Zero, and Growth through Collaboration—with his natural curiosity, these methods become the game-changers needed to move businesses toward exponential enterprise value growth.

This talent, what some call his highest value role, has opened the doors for Chad to work directly with leaders of businesses of every size across every industry. By analyzing the various aspects of an organization's friction, Chad can quickly identify invisible opportunities that enable companies to create competitive advantages and increase margins, resulting in exponential enterprise value growth. The result is a proven track record of over forty owned or previously owned high-growth companies and hundreds of Growth Partnerships across North America.

Now focused on helping others, he has passed on leadership in each of his companies and operates solely in his Unique

Ability through Growth Collaboration Partnerships and the SEEDSPARK Growth Academy.

Chad advises business leaders to stay curious and look for the friction in their own businesses to remove competition, name their price, and go global through collaboration. If you need help Removing the Film or Just Adding a Zero, contact Chad to discuss 100X Collaborations at SeedSpark.com.

Ready to turn your frictions into *fuel?*

DOWNLOAD THE FREE TOOL!

FRICTIONFUEL.COM

CoLAB

Join the Leading Global Entrepreneur Collaboration Platform!

Unlock your potential with a dynamic platform where entrepreneurs connect, collaborate, and grow.

GET STARTED AT:
SEEDSPARK.COM/COLAB

Want to Learn More About the Author?

CHADTJENKINS.COM

SEEDSPARK
GROWTH PARTNERS

Outperform
your competition
and become a
category of one.

WANT TO ADD A ZERO?

Learn how to remove the film, outperform your competition, and grow exponentially through collaboration.

TAKE THE ASSESSMENT TODAY

JUSTADDZERO.COM

THIS BOOK IS PROTECTED INTELLECTUAL PROPERTY

Instant IP™

The author of this book values Intellectual Property. The book you just read is protected by Instant IP™, a proprietary process, which integrates blockchain technology giving Intellectual Property "Global Protection." By creating a "Time-Stamped" smart contract that can never be tampered with or changed, we establish "First Use" that tracks back to the author.

Instant IP™ functions much like a Pre-Patent™ since it provides an immutable "First Use" of the Intellectual Property. This is achieved through our proprietary process of leveraging blockchain technology and smart contracts. As a result, proving "First Use" is simple through a global and verifiable smart contract. By protecting intellectual property with blockchain technology and smart contracts, we establish a "First to File" event.

Protected by Instant IP™

LEARN MORE AT INSTANTIP.TODAY